YOUNG PEOPLE OF THE BIBLE

the very special pres

Text by
BETTY SMITH
Art by
NORM HAMDORF

LUTTERWORTH PRESS
GUILDFORD AND LONDON

First British Edition 1980
Copyright © 1978 Lutheran Publishing House, Adelaide.
Printed in Hong Kong

What was that noise? Old Eli lifted his head and glanced sharply around. Everything had been very quiet in God's house at Shiloh. The curtains hung in soft folds. The candle flames were straight and still. Even with the extra people who had come for the great yearly festival, all was just as it should be — peaceful and reverent.

Suddenly the same noise broke the quietness again — the sound of a woman sobbing. Eli stood up and looked around. There it was again. Who could be crying so bitterly? Then he saw a woman kneeling some distance away.

As he walked across, Eli felt angry with her for making a scene. He even thought she had been drinking. But,

when he saw her face, he knew he was
wrong. This woman was dreadfully
unhappy.

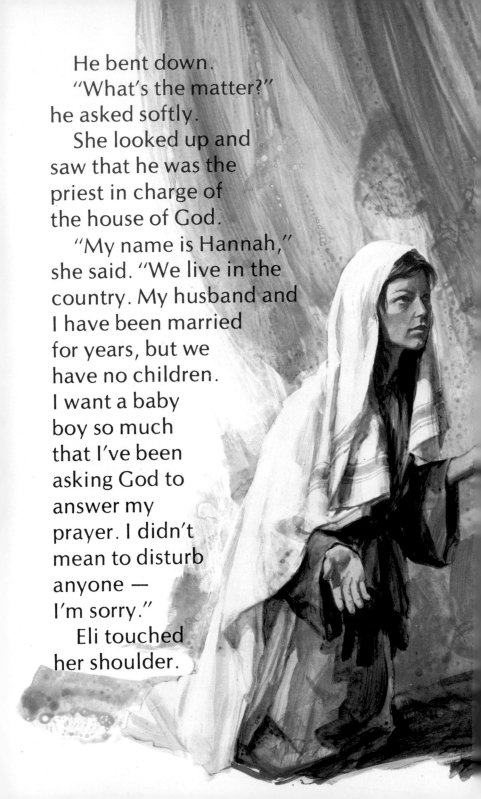

He bent down.

"What's the matter?" he asked softly.

She looked up and saw that he was the priest in charge of the house of God.

"My name is Hannah," she said. "We live in the country. My husband and I have been married for years, but we have no children. I want a baby boy so much that I've been asking God to answer my prayer. I didn't mean to disturb anyone — I'm sorry."

Eli touched her shoulder.

"Don't be sorry — that is what God's house is for; and the sound of the prayers of people should never disturb anyone. I do hope that your wish comes true."

"I'm sure that this time God will grant my wish," Hannah said. "If I do have a son, I've promised that I will do all I can to see that he grows up to love and serve the Lord."

"And may He bless you as you journey home," Eli said. "Go in peace."

As Hannah
left Shiloh,
she knew
in her heart
that this time all
would be well.
And it was. Next
year, when everyone
else from Hannah's house
went up to the yearly service,
she stayed at home. For now
she had her baby son, and he was
too tiny to travel. Hannah often
held him close to her and
whispered, "Thank you, God."
Then she would ask
Him to bless little
Samuel and keep
him strong and well.

For three years,
Hannah missed the
service. Then it was
time to keep her
promise.

One day, Eli saw a woman coming
toward him. She held a small boy by
the hand.

"Do you remember me?" she began;
"I'm the woman you spoke to some
years ago here, when I was crying."

Eli did remember, for it had been a
very unusual thing to happen.

"I told you then," Hannah said, "that
if I did have a son, I had promised I
would do all I could to see that he was
brought up to love and serve God. Now
I've kept that promise. I have brought

Samuel here so that you may train him to be a priest like yourself — someone whose special work is to show others how best they may worship and serve God."

Eli smiled and looked kindly at the little, dark-haired boy.

"You're quite sure that this is what you want?" he asked Hannah.

She looked lovingly at her small son. It was not easy to let him go. But a promise was a promise, and she must keep faith with God who had made her prayer came true.

"Yes," she answered Eli. "You'll look after him, won't you?"

"Of course we will," Eli comforted her. "Don't worry."

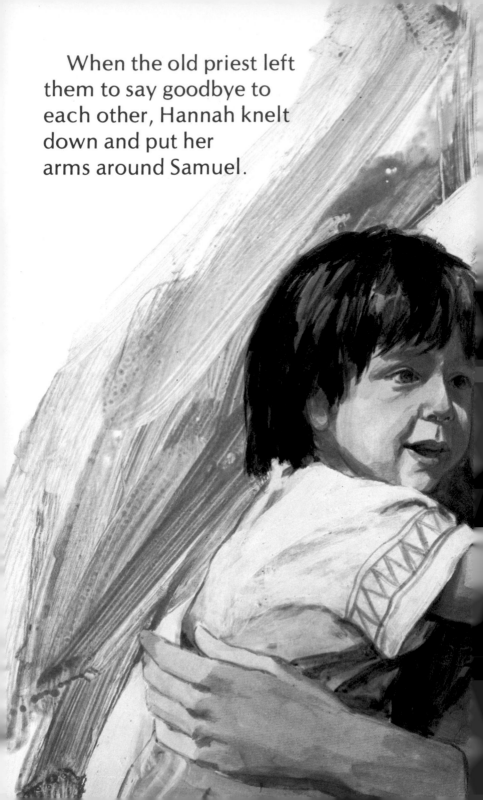

When the old priest left
them to say goodbye to
each other, Hannah knelt
down and put her
arms around Samuel.

"My little, little son! You will be good, won't you? Learn all you can. Mother and Father won't forget you, even though we are parted from you."

Samuel felt afraid, but he tried not to show it.

"That's a good boy!" said his mother. "Every year when we come to the service, I'll see you. I'll bring you lots of presents and — (whispering in his ear) there'll be one special one."

Samuel looked at her without speaking. She saw he was trying not to cry.

"That's my brave boy!" she said, although she felt like crying herself. "Remember, you're never alone. God is always with you." And with a final hug, she was gone.

How different from home everything seemed to Samuel! Imagine living always in a great big church! Of course, there were other little boys there, too, all growing up to be priests.

What did they do all day?

Well, first of all, they
had to learn to read and
write. They were taught from the books
(or scrolls) of the Bible, the holy Book
written by men to whom God gave His
message in words for all to hear. The

boys had to learn many verses off by heart. There were special hymns and psalms to be learnt, too, for singing at the various services. They also ran messages for the older priests. They kept the lamps filled with oil. They placed new candles in their holders. They helped to keep everything clean by sweeping and dusting (which they didn't like very much). Like all boys, they played together, and learnt to give and take. There was so much to do that the days passed very quickly.

But the night time!
Everything was so
dark and different then, as Samuel lay
on his sleeping-mat. That was the time
when he thought most about his own
home and the people he loved.

And, a long way away, Hannah was
also thinking of him. Never a day

passed that she did not ask God to bless her son, so that he would grow up to be faithful to God. As years went by, Hannah and her husband had more children, but she never, never forgot Samuel. Each year she worked for weeks on that very special present for him. What do you think it was?

Hannah gathered the finest, softest wool from the sheep, and spun it into creamy thread. After that, she made a coat from the thread, to reach from Samuel's neck to his knees. Some of the wool she dyed to make a design all around the edge, with a pattern of fruit, or perhaps grape leaves. One year the coat itself might be dyed a soft blue. Another year, the coat might be cream, like the wool itself.

Every time Hannah
attended the yearly
festival, she took a
new coat with her.
Samuel was growing quickly;
last year's coat was
far too short. How eagerly Samuel
would watch for his mother!

Down the hill he would run to meet her, his arms stretched wide. And Hannah, too, would hurry as fast as she could. Her hands would be full of little parcels — all for him. Raisins, figs, honey, cakes — and, of course, the one very special present, lovingly wrapped. Hannah was glad to see her son becoming tall and strong. She would hold up the new bigger and longer coat she had made, and measure it against him. Would it be too big? No, it was just right.

Samuel had so much to tell his mother — all about the new lessons he was learning, the new things he had found, the new ways of serving God which he had been taught. One year, he had something so wonderful to tell her that he almost whispered it.

"I was lying on my mat asleep," he said, "when I heard a voice calling: Samuel! Samuel!"

"What did you do?" asked Hannah.

"I thought it was Eli. But when I ran to his room, he hadn't called. So I went and lay down again."

"Did you hear the voice any more?" asked Hannah.

"Yes, just the same; and Eli again said that he hadn't spoken. When it happened the third time and I went to

him, he told me — oh, Mother," and his voice sank lower still, "he told me that it must be God Himself calling me. He said to lie down and if I heard the voice again, I should reply, 'Speak, Lord, I'm listening'."

Hannah caught his hands between her own.

"And did you hear it, Samuel?"

"Yes, yes, I did! So I said what Eli told me to say. And then — God spoke to me, Mother, to *me*! He told me something that would happen in the future, which I have repeated only to Eli. Isn't that wonderful!"

Hannah couldn't speak. Samuel had altered in many ways, but his mother's love would never change. She knew now that her son would one day be a

prophet. Through Samuel, God would tell his people how they could truly serve Him. Because she had kept her promise, everyone in that country would have the chance to serve God in faith, love, and trust.